HOW TO START A COFFEE TRUCK

A Step by Step Successful Guide to open and starting a profitable Business

James Brian

Table of Contents

Chapter 1
Brew Up Your Dream: Concept & Planning - A Deep Dive

The aroma of freshly brewed coffee is more than just a delightful scent; it's a beacon of potential, a siren song calling out to the entrepreneurial spirit. If you're captivated by the idea of bringing that joy to others through your own mobile coffee haven, you've embarked on an exciting journey! Chapter 1 of "How to Start a Coffee Truck" lays the groundwork for your cafe on wheels, guiding you through the crucial process of defining your concept and setting a strong foundation for success.

1.1 Unveiling Your Coffee Vision

Before you hunt for the perfect truck or invest in your first bag of beans, take a moment to brew up your vision. This is where you answer the question, "What makes my coffee truck unique?"

- *Define your niche:* Will you be the caffeine companion for busy professionals, the fuel for a bustling farmers' market, or the oasis for bookworms in a cozy park? Identifying your target audience and their needs will inform everything from your menu to your location.

- *Craft your identity:* What personality will your coffee truck exude? Are you a vintage charmer, a sleek minimalist, or a vibrant splash of color? Your branding and design should tell a story and resonate with your target audience.

- *Identify your unique selling points*: What will set you apart from the competition? Do you offer ethically sourced beans, innovative brewing methods, or handcrafted pastries? Find your niche and shine a spotlight on what makes you special.

1.2 Charting Your Course: The Business Plan Blueprint

A well-crafted business plan is your roadmap to success. It's not just a requirement for potential investors; it's a tool for clarity, organization, and financial prudence.

- *Market research:* Dive into the world of coffee trucks! Understand your local market, including existing competitors, customer preferences, and pricing trends. This data will guide your decisions and help you avoid common pitfalls.

- *Financial projections:* Crunch the numbers! Estimate your start-up costs, equipment investments, operating expenses, and potential revenue. Be realistic, factor in seasonality, and create a financial model that reflects your unique concept.

- *Target locations:* Where will your coffee magic unfold? Research high-traffic areas, explore permit limitations, and identify partnerships with local businesses or events to maximize your customer reach.

1.3 Legalities & Licenses: Navigating the Maze

The world of food trucks involves regulations and permits. Don't let paperwork dampen your enthusiasm; consider it an essential step towards a safe and compliant operation.

- *Business permits:* Understand your local business licensing requirements and obtain the necessary permits to operate legally. This might include health department permits, vendor licenses, and mobile food permits.

- *Health regulations:* Food safety is paramount. Familiarize yourself with health regulations specific to mobile food vendors and implement robust cleaning and sanitation practices.
- *Insurance coverage:* Protect your investment and your customers with appropriate insurance coverage, including liability insurance and vehicle insurance.

Brewing Beyond Basics:

Think of this as the foundation of your coffee kingdom. Remember, these are just the initial steps, and there's plenty of room for customization and creativity.

- *Sustainability and ethics:* Consider sourcing your beans from ethical farms and using eco-friendly practices to minimize your environmental impact. This resonates with today's conscious consumers and aligns with your brand values.

- *Community connections:* Coffee trucks are more than just a caffeine dispenser; they can be community hubs. Partner with local businesses, participate in events, and foster a welcoming atmosphere for your customers.

- *Tech-savvy solutions:* Embrace technology! Explore point-of-sale systems, mobile payment options, and social media to streamline operations, engage customers, and build a loyal following.

Remember, your coffee truck is an extension of your passion. Inject your personality, embrace your unique vision, and let your enthusiasm flow into every cup you serve. As you navigate, focus on building a strong foundation, but don't be afraid to dream big and envision the magic your coffee truck will bring to the world.

Chapter 2

Finding Your Perfect Bean: Sourcing & Equipment - Mastering the Essentials

As your coffee truck dreams start to solidify, Chapter 2 takes you on a deep dive into the heart of the matter - the very soul of your mobile oasis: the coffee itself. From sourcing the finest beans to equipping your chariot with the right tools, this chapter is your guide to crafting the perfect cup on wheels.

2.1 Sourcing Supreme Sips: A Bean Voyage

Your coffee's flavor journey begins not in your truck, but at the origin - the soil where the beans were nurtured. Choosing the right suppliers and beans sets the stage for everything you create.

- *Bean origin and varieties:* Explore the world of coffee! From the bright acidity of Ethiopian Yirgacheffe to the deep chocolate notes of Guatemalan Antigua, delve into different origins and varietals to discover flavors that align with your concept.

- *Sourcing with ethics:* Go beyond taste and seek ethically sourced beans. Fair trade, organic, and direct trade options ensure sustainable practices and empower farmers, adding a feel-good dimension to your coffee.

- *Freshness is king:* Prioritize freshness! Look for roasters who source directly, roast in small batches, and have a fast turnaround time. Stale beans will never translate to exceptional coffee.

2.2 Gearing Up for Greatness: Your Coffee Arsenal

Now it's time to equip your truck with the tools of the trade! Whether you're a latte art maestro or a pour-over aficionado, the right equipment ensures consistency and quality.

- *Espresso Machine*: The heart of your operation! Choose a machine that fits your budget, volume needs, and desired beverage offerings. From compact automatic machines to high-end commercial options, consider factors like steam wand power, brew head type, and ease of maintenance.

- *Grinder*: Precise grind, perfect taste! Invest in a quality grinder that ensures consistent particle size for optimal extraction. Burr grinders offer superior control, while some espresso machines may come with built-in grinders.

- *Brewers:* Beyond espresso! Depending on your menu, you might want additional brewing methods like pour-over cones, cold brew towers, or automatic drip brewers. Each method offers unique flavor profiles and caters to different preferences.

Beyond the Essentials:

Your equipment choices go beyond just functionality. They enhance your workflow, brand identity, and overall customer experience.

- *Mobile-friendly equipment:* Choose compact, efficient machines designed for the rigors of a mobile environment. Look for features like water tanks, portable power options, and easy cleaning for smooth day-to-day operations.

- *Sustainable choices:* Consider energy-efficient equipment and eco-friendly practices. Reusable filters, biodegradable cups, and energy-saving features can minimize your environmental footprint and resonate with conscious customers.
- *Aesthetics matter:* Let your equipment reflect your brand! Choose machines with colors and styles that complement your overall design, creating a cohesive and attractive experience for your customers.

2.3 Powering Your Brew: Fueling the Coffee Magic

Your mobile haven needs a reliable source of power to keep the coffee flowing. Understanding your options and planning ahead ensures uninterrupted service and a smooth operation.

- *Generator power*: Invest in a quiet, fuel-efficient generator that can handle your equipment's electricity requirements. Consider generator size, runtime, and fuel capacity to ensure you have enough juice for a full day's service.

- *Battery power:* A sustainable alternative! Explore lithium-ion battery systems designed for mobile food vendors. These offer quieter operation, reduced emissions, and portability, but may require careful planning to manage battery life.

- *External power hookups:* Look for locations that offer access to external power sources, eliminating the need for generators or batteries and simplifying your setup.

Brewing Beyond Basics:

Remember, equipment is just a tool. Your skill and passion are what bring it to life.

- *Maintenance matters:* Regularly clean and maintain your equipment to ensure optimal performance and longevity. Learn basic troubleshooting techniques to address minor issues and keep your coffee flowing.

- *Experiment and refine:* Don't be afraid to experiment with different brewing methods and tweak recipes to find the perfect cup. Your taste buds and customers will thank you for the continuous improvement.

- *Train your baristas*: Invest in barista training or develop your own skills to master coffee preparation, latte art, and customer interaction. Skilled baristas are the driving force behind a successful coffee truck.

This chapter has equipped you with the knowledge and tools to source the finest beans and find the perfect equipment for your mobile coffee haven. Remember, quality craftsmanship, a focus on fresh ingredients, and a touch of your own creativity will brew up the magic that keeps your customers coming back for more. As you navigate this crucial chapter, keep your vision close, your taste buds engaged, and your spirit adventurous.

Chapter 3
Building Your Coffee Castle: Vehicle & Design - Your Mobile Masterpiece

Chapter 3 takes you on a whirlwind tour of your coffee truck's physical domain – the vessel that will carry your dream to the streets. From choosing the perfect chariot to crafting a welcoming and aesthetically pleasing space, this chapter is your guide to building a mobile masterpiece that reflects your brand and delights your customers.

3.1 Choosing Your Chariot: Mobile Canvas Options

Your coffee truck is more than just a mode of transportation; it's an extension of your brand, a statement piece, and an inviting haven for caffeine enthusiasts. Choosing the right vehicle sets the stage for everything to come.

- *Food trucks:* The classic choice! Trucks offer ample space for equipment, storage, and customer interaction. Explore options like step vans, box trucks, or even vintage vehicles for a unique vibe.

- *Trailers:* A versatile option! Towable trailers offer flexibility and can be detached when parked, but may require additional setup and space considerations.

- *Vans:* Compact and convenient! Vans are ideal for tight spaces and offer a streamlined operation, though internal workspace might be limited.

- *Specialty vehicles*: Think outside the box! From converted rickshaws to vintage scooters, unique vehicles can create a distinct brand identity and attract attention.

Beyond the Basics:
Choosing a vehicle goes beyond size and functionality. Consider these factors for a perfect match:

- *Budget:* Set a realistic budget and factor in purchase price, customization costs, ongoing maintenance, and fuel efficiency.

- *Permits and regulations:* Ensure your chosen vehicle complies with local size and weight limitations for mobile food vendors.

- *Brand alignment:* Your vehicle should reflect your brand personality. Choose a style that complements your logo, color scheme, and overall aesthetic.

- *Customer experience:* Think about customer flow and comfort. Will there be enough space for ordering, waiting, and enjoying coffee? Can you incorporate seating or standing areas?

3.2 Crafting Your Coffee Canvas: Design & Branding

Now comes the fun part - transforming your blank canvas into a coffee wonderland! Your design should tell a story, attract customers, and create a memorable experience.

- *Exterior design:* Let your colors sing! Choose eye-catching paint schemes, vinyl graphics, or murals that reflect your brand and menu. Don't forget signage that clearly communicates your name and offerings.

- *Interior design:* Create a welcoming atmosphere! Consider lighting, seating arrangements, storage solutions, and countertop space for barista magic. Incorporate your brand colors and materials for a cohesive feel.

- *Functional touches:* Design for efficiency! Optimize the layout for smooth workflow, prioritize easy access to equipment and supplies, and incorporate features like sinks, hand washing stations, and waste disposal.

Beyond the Basics: Think of your design as an extension of your brand storytelling.

- *Theme and personality:* Inject your unique flair! Are you a vintage charmer, a minimalist haven, or a playful pop of color? Let your theme guide your design choices.

- *Lighting and ambience:* Set the mood! Warm lighting creates a cozy feel, while natural light and open spaces can be invigorating. Experiment with different types of lighting to enhance the atmosphere.

- *Sensory experience:* Engage all senses! Play music that aligns with your brand, incorporate pleasing aromas (think freshly brewed coffee or pastries), and use comfortable materials for seating and surfaces.

3.3 Tech & Tools for Efficiency: Stepping into the Future

In today's digital age, embracing technology can streamline your operations and enhance the customer experience.

- *Point-of-sale (POS) systems*: Invest in a user-friendly POS system that allows for quick order taking, payment processing, and inventory management. Consider mobile payment options for added convenience.

- *Inventory management tools:* Stay organized! Utilize apps or software to track your inventory levels, order supplies efficiently, and avoid running out of essential ingredients.

- *Customer engagement tools:* Build loyalty! Explore loyalty programs, social media marketing, and email campaigns to connect with your customers, offer promotions, and gather feedback.

Beyond the Basics:

Technology can be your secret weapon for a smooth and successful operation.

- *Data analytics*: Utilize the data provided by your POS system and other tools to understand customer preferences, track sales trends, and optimize your menu and offerings.

- *Sustainability solutions*: Explore eco-friendly options like digital receipts, reusable cups, and solar panels to minimize your environmental impact and appeal to conscious customers.

- *Staying connected:* Invest in reliable internet connectivity to facilitate online ordering, social media interactions, and real-time communication with your team.

Remember, your coffee truck is a living, breathing entity. Be open to adaptation and improvement as you go.

Gather feedback: Listen to your customers! Their suggestions and preferences can help you refine your design, menu ...and service offerings. Host customer surveys, encourage open communication, and actively seek feedback to keep your coffee truck evolving.

3.4 Building Community beyond Your Wheels

Your coffee truck can be more than just a caffeine provider; it can be a community hub, a gathering place for laughter and connection. Here's how:

- *Partner with local businesses:* Collaborate with neighboring shops, galleries, or event organizers to host joint events, offer special promotions, and cross-promote each other's businesses.

- *Support local initiatives:* Get involved in your community! Sponsor local sports teams, participate in charity events, or offer discounts to students or seniors. This fosters goodwill and builds a loyal customer base.

- *Embrace pop-up opportunities:* Don't limit yourself to one location! Explore pop-up opportunities at festivals, markets, or corporate events to expand your reach and attract new customers.

Remember, the heart of your coffee truck lies in the human connection.

- *Create a welcoming atmosphere:* Be friendly, approachable, and engage with your customers. Build rapport, remember their names, and personalize your interactions.
- *Host events and workshops:* Organize coffee cupping sessions, barista demonstrations, or even open mic nights to create a dynamic and engaging space for your community.

- *Celebrate your passions:* Don't just sell coffee, share your love for it! Offer coffee brewing tips, educate customers about different origins and varietals, and create a coffee-centric experience that goes beyond the cup.

This chapter has equipped you with the tools and inspiration to transform your mobile canvas into a coffee masterpiece. From choosing the perfect chariot to crafting a welcoming and efficient space, remember to let your brand identity shine through, embrace technology for a seamless operation, and build a community around your coffee haven.

As you pour your passion into every detail, your mobile coffee oasis will become a cherished destination for caffeine enthusiasts and a vibrant hub for meaningful connections. So, roll up your sleeves, unleash your creativity, and get ready to brew up a community that thrives on every delicious cup.

With a detailed breakdown of vehicle choices, design tips, and community-building strategies, you're well-equipped to transform your vision into a reality that delights your customers and fuels your entrepreneurial spirit. Remember, the journey doesn't end here – keep the coffee flowing, the music playing, and the connections thriving, and your mobile masterpiece will become a beacon of joy and deliciousness in your community.

Chapter 4
Mastering the Coffee Craft: Barista Training & Recipes - From Bean to Bliss

Chapter 4 marks a pivotal turning point in your coffee truck saga. It takes you beyond the wheels and equipment, delving into the heart and soul of the operation: brewing the perfect cup. From mastering the art of coffee preparation to crafting signature beverages and ensuring consistent quality, this chapter equips you with the knowledge and skills to transform those humble beans into liquid bliss.

4.1 From Bean to Barista: Mastering the Espresso Symphony

Whether you choose to wield the steaming wand yourself or entrust your coffee alchemy to a team of skilled baristas, understanding the basics of espresso preparation is essential.

- *Espresso extraction*: It's all about the grind! Learn to dial in the perfect grind size and tamping pressure for optimal extraction, resulting in a balanced espresso full of flavor and crema.

- *Milk frothing and texturing:* Steam with confidence! Master the art of creating silky smooth microfoam, essential for latte art and adding body to milk-based beverages.

- *Cleaning and maintenance:* Keep your machine purring! Develop a consistent cleaning and maintenance routine for your espresso machine and grinder to ensure hygiene and optimal performance.
Beyond the Basics:

Become a true coffee maestro by delving deeper into the science and artistry of espresso brewing.

- *Water quality:* Water is the hidden hero! Understand the importance of using filtered, low-mineral water for consistent extraction and avoid the pitfalls of off-tasting coffee.

- *Temperature control:* Keep it cool! Maintain proper brewing and steaming temperatures for optimal extraction and milk texturing. Experiment with different temperature variations to fine-tune your signature style.

- *Grinder calibration:* Precision is key! Learn to adjust your grinder settings for different beans and roast levels, ensuring consistent grind size and extraction.

4.2 Crafting the Perfect Cup: Recipe Innovation & Exploration

Your menu is your canvas, and your coffee the paint. In Chapter 4, you'll learn to concoct irresistible beverages that reflect your brand and tantalize your customers' taste buds.

- *Classic espresso-based drinks:* Master the basics! Latte, cappuccino, macchiato, flat white – learn the ratios, techniques, and presentation styles for these timeless favorites.

- *Signature creations*: Get creative! Develop unique beverages that reflect your brand and appeal to your target audience. Experiment with flavor combinations, syrups, spices, and garnishes to craft your own coffee masterpieces.

- *Seasonal adaptations:* Keep it fresh! Introduce seasonal variations to your menu, featuring ingredients like pumpkin spice in fall, peppermint in winter, or refreshing fruit flavors in summer.

Beyond the Basics:

Go beyond the standard cafe fare and elevate your coffee offerings to new heights.

- *Cold brew magic:* Master the art of cold brew preparation, offering a smooth, low-acidity alternative to hot coffee. Explore nitro infusion for a creamy, cascading experience.

- *Pour-over precision*: Embrace the slow pour! Train your baristas in the art of pour-over brewing, offering customers a nuanced and flavorful coffee experience.
- *Tea and beyond:* Expand your horizons! Consider offering a selection of teas, hot chocolate, or even blended milk drinks to cater to a wider range of preferences.

4.3 Quality Control & Consistency: From Sip to Savor

Consistency is king in the coffee kingdom. Chapter 4 provides the tools and techniques to ensure every cup served is a symphony of perfect flavor and presentation.

- *Standardized recipes*: Develop standard recipes for all your beverages, specifying ingredients, ratios, and preparation methods. Train your baristas to follow these recipes precisely for consistent quality.
- *Regular calibration and cleaning:* Maintain your equipment! Regularly calibrate your grinder and espresso machine, and implement a rigorous cleaning and sanitation routine to ensure hygienic and optimal performance.

- *Taste buds as allies:* Train your taste buds! Practice regular coffee cupping sessions to develop your palate and ensure consistent quality control of your brews.

Beyond the Basics:

Consistency goes beyond just the beverage itself. Create a customer experience that's as reliable and pleasurable as your coffee.

- *Visual presentation:* Make it look as good as it tastes! Train your baristas in latte art techniques, proper cup handling, and attractive garnish presentation.
- *Customer service excellence:* Smile and serve! Cultivate a welcoming and efficient service environment. Train your baristas to be friendly, knowledgeable, and efficient, creating a positive customer experience every time.
- *Quality ingredients:* Don't skimp on the good stuff! Use high-quality beans, fresh milk, and top-notch syrups and spices to guarantee a premium coffee experience.

Remember, the art of coffee brewing is a continuous journey of learning and refinement.

Seek out training: Invest in barista training for yourself and your team. Attend workshops, participate in competitions, and seek mentorship from experienced professionals to hone your skills and stay ahead of the curve.

- *Experiment and iterate:* Don't be afraid to experiment! Try new coffee origins, explore alternative brewing methods, and solicit feedback from your customers to refine your recipes and menu offerings.

- *Embrace feedback and adapt*: Be open to constructive criticism and suggestions. Use customer feedback to identify areas for improvement and continually adapt your offerings to remain relevant and exciting.

Chapter 4 has equipped you with the knowledge and skills to transform your coffee truck into a haven of delectable brews and barista artistry.

From mastering espresso extraction to crafting signature beverages and ensuring consistent quality, this chapter is your foundation for brewing coffee mastery. Remember, practice makes perfect, so grab your tamper, unleash your creativity, and let the espresso symphony begin. As you pour passion into every cup, your coffee truck will become a celebrated destination for caffeine connoisseurs and a testament to your commitment to crafting liquid bliss, one bean at a time.

Chapter 5
Finding Your Coffee Crowd: Marketing & Location - From Beans to Buzz

Chapter 5 marks the crucial transition from your carefully crafted cafe on wheels to the vibrant world of customers and community. In this chapter, you'll learn how to navigate the dynamic intersection of marketing and location, attracting your ideal audience and finding the perfect spots to set your coffee chariot ablaze.

5.1 Branding Your Brew: Building a Buzzing Identity

Your brand is your voice, your story, your beacon in the crowded coffee landscape. You'll discover how to build a unique and compelling identity that resonates with your target customers.

- *Crafting your story:* What makes you different? Define your brand's core values, personality, and mission. Are you the adventurous explorer, the vintage charmer, or the eco-conscious crusader?

- *Visual storytelling:* Let your colors sing! Develop a distinct logo, color palette, and visual style that reflects your brand story and attracts your target audience.

- *Voice and messaging:* Find your tone! Create consistent messaging across all your channels, whether it's playful, informative, or inspiring, ensuring your brand personality shines through.

Beyond the Basics: Think beyond just aesthetics. Your brand extends to every customer touch point.

- *Website and social media:* Build your online presence! Create a user-friendly website and active social media profiles showcasing your menu, location, brand story, and customer interactions.

- *Promotional materials:* Make it irresistible! Design flyers, posters, and menus that reflect your brand and entice customers to try your coffee. Consider eco-friendly options like recycled paper or digital menus.

- *Partnerships and collaborations:* Team up for success! Partner with local businesses, organizations, or events to cross-promote and expand your reach.

5.2 Locating Your Loyal Beans: Finding the Perfect Pitch

Location, location, location! You'll learn how to identify the ideal spots to park your coffee truck and cultivate a loyal customer base.

- *Target audience analysis:* Know your beans! Understand your ideal customer's demographics, daily routines, and preferred locations. Research areas with high foot traffic or businesses that complement your brand.

- *Permits and regulations:* Navigate the maze! Research local regulations regarding mobile food vendors, permitting requirements, and parking restrictions in your target locations.

- *Testing and adapting*: Be flexible! Experiment with different locations, monitor foot traffic and sales, and adapt your schedule and location strategy based on your findings.

Beyond the Basics:
Think beyond the obvious. Explore creative ways to expand your reach and connect with your audience.

- *Pop-up opportunities:* Don't stay parked! Participate in festivals, markets, corporate events, or even private functions to create temporary buzz and reach new customers.

- *Delivery options:* Cater to convenience! Consider offering delivery services through apps or partnerships with local businesses to cater to busy coffee lovers.

- *Subscription models:* Build loyalty! Explore subscription services offering weekly or monthly coffee deliveries, exclusive discounts, or early access to new menu items.

5.3 Marketing Your Magic: Engaging Your Tribe

You'll discover how to leverage the power of marketing to turn casual customers into passionate fans.

- *Social media engagement:* Spark a conversation! Share captivating content on your social media channels, featuring behind-the-scenes glimpses, customer testimonials, and delicious coffee visuals. Run contests and promotions to encourage interaction.

- *Loyalty programs:* Reward the faithful! Implement a loyalty program that rewards repeat customers with discounts, free drinks, or exclusive perks. This incentivizes loyalty and builds a strong community around your brand.

- *Email marketing:* Stay connected! Build an email list and send engaging newsletters featuring promotions, new menu items, or even personalized birthday wishes. Cultivate a direct relationship with your customers.

Beyond the Basics:

Go beyond traditional marketing and create lasting connections with your community.

- *Community events:* Be a good neighbor! Host coffee cupping sessions, barista workshops, or open mic nights at your truck. Participate in local events and support community initiatives.

- *Customer feedback:* Listen and learn! Encourage customers to provide feedback through surveys, social media mentions, or open conversations. Use this feedback to improve your offerings and build stronger relationships.

- *Collaborations and influencer partnerships*: Team up with the trendsetters! Partner with local influencers, bloggers, or food enthusiasts to promote your coffee truck and reach a wider audience.

Remember, marketing is an ongoing process. Track your results, learn from your mistakes, and adapt your strategies to reach your target audience effectively. As you consistently deliver delicious coffee, engage with your community, and build a strong brand identity, your coffee truck will become a magnet for coffee lovers, creating a loyal following and a vibrant hub for caffeine-fueled connections.

Chapter 5 has equipped you with the tools and tactics to navigate the dynamic world of coffee marketing and location strategy. From crafting a captivating brand identity to finding the perfect pitch for your mobile haven, this chapter empowers you to attract your ideal customers and cultivate a loyal coffee tribe. Remember, the key lies in authenticity, community engagement, and a relentless pursuit of deliciousness. As you build your presence, hone your marketing game, and connect with your audience, your coffee truck will become more than just a mobile cafe; it will become a thriving social hub and a cherished destination for coffee connoisseurs and community enthusiasts alike.

With a detailed breakdown of brand building, location strategies, and engaging marketing tactics, you're well-equipped to turn your coffee dreams into a bustling reality. Remember, the journey doesn't end here – keep the social media buzzing, the location maps updated, and the community connections thriving, and your mobile coffee oasis will become a beacon of deliciousness and connection in your community.

So, roll up your sleeves, unleash your marketing magic, and find your perfect pitch. The world of coffee awaits, ready to be brewed into a thriving business and a community hub fueled by passion, flavor, and the spirit of connection. Bon voyage, coffee adventurer! Your mobile masterpiece awaits.

Chapter 6
Brewing Beyond Beans: Operations & Finances - From Hustle to Harmony

Chapter 6 marks a pivotal shift in your mobile coffee odyssey. As you've crafted your menu, honed your skills, and found your audience, it's time to delve into the operational and financial realm, ensuring your coffee haven runs smoothly and sustainably. From mastering daily routines to navigating the financial currents, this chapter equips you with the tools and knowledge to transform your passion into a thriving business.

6.1 Daily Grind Symphony: Operational Efficiency & Flow

Running a coffee truck is a dynamic dance of preparation, customer interaction, and cleaning. Here, you'll learn to orchestrate this daily symphony with efficiency and ease.

- *Pre-opening routine:* Set the stage for success! Develop a pre-opening checklist that covers stocking supplies, calibrating equipment, brewing fresh pots, and setting up your coffee oasis. Consistency and efficiency are key.

- *Customer flow and service:* Be the maestro of caffeine satisfaction! Implement a streamlined order-taking and coffee preparation process to minimize wait times and maximize customer satisfaction. Consider contactless payment options for added convenience.

- *Closing procedures:* Secure the brew! Establish a closing routine for cleaning equipment, restocking supplies, secure cash handling, and leaving the mobile masterpiece ready for the next day's adventure.

Beyond the Basics:
Think beyond routine tasks and create a work environment that fosters teamwork and joy.

- *Training and communication:* Invest in your team! Train your baristas on equipment operation, coffee preparation, customer service, and safety procedures. Open communication keeps everyone on the same page.

- *Inventory management:* Be the bean maestro! Develop a system for tracking inventory levels, ordering supplies efficiently, and minimizing waste. Utilize technology like inventory management apps for real-time updates and better control.

- *Health and safety:* Prioritize well-being! Implement and enforce strict hygiene and safety protocols, including food handling procedures, equipment sanitation, and emergency response guidelines.

6.2 Financial Alchemy: Brewing Profits & Navigating Numbers

This equips you with the financial literacy to transform your coffee passion into a profitable venture.

- *Pricing strategy:* Find the sweet spot! Analyze your costs, research competitor pricing, and consider your target audience to determine optimal pricing for your menu items. Don't undercut your value, but remain competitive.

- *Cost control:* Be penny-wise, pound-foolish! Track your expenses, identify areas for cost reduction, and negotiate with suppliers for better deals. Every penny saved contributes to the bottom line.

- *Financial recordkeeping:* Stay organized! Implement a system for recording daily sales, expenses, inventory levels, and payroll. Utilize accounting software or spreadsheets for accurate and efficient recordkeeping.

Beyond the Basics:
Go beyond basic calculations and embrace financial planning for long-term success.

- *Business plan and projections:* Chart your course! Revisit your initial business plan and update financial projections based on your actual sales and expenses. This helps you monitor progress, adapt strategies, and secure future funding.

- *Taxes and permits:* Navigate the maze! Understand your local tax regulations for mobile food vendors and ensure you comply with all necessary permits and licenses. Seek professional guidance if needed.

- *Insurance and risk management:* Be prepared! Invest in appropriate insurance coverage to protect your business from unforeseen events like vehicle breakdowns, equipment damage, or liability claims.

Remember, financial management is an ongoing process. Adapt your strategies as your business evolves, seek professional advice when needed, and celebrate your financial milestones.

- *Analyze and adapt:* Keep your finger on the pulse! Regularly analyze your sales data, customer feedback, and competitor trends to identify areas for improvement and adapt your pricing, menu, and operational strategies accordingly.

- *Embrace continuous learning:* Stay informed! Attend workshops, participate in online courses, and network with other entrepreneurs to learn new financial management strategies and keep up with industry trends.

- *Invest in automation:* Explore technology! Consider digital payment systems, online ordering platforms, or inventory management software to streamline operations, reduce errors, and free up your time for other aspects of your business.

This chapter has equipped you with the tools and knowledge to navigate the operational and financial aspects of your mobile coffee haven. From orchestrating the daily grind to mastering financial alchemy, this chapter empowers you to transform your passion into a sustainable and profitable business.

Remember, efficiency, planning, and adaptability are key. As you hone your operational skills, manage your finances with wisdom, and embrace continuous learning, your coffee truck will become a testament to your entrepreneurial spirit and a source of delicious fuel for your community.

With a detailed breakdown of daily routines, inventory management techniques, and financial planning tools, you're well-equipped to turn your coffee dreams into a smoothly running reality. Remember, the journey doesn't end here – keep the coffee flowing, the inventory optimized, and the financial records accurate, and your mobile masterpiece will become a haven of efficiency and profitability.

So, put on your barista apron, sharpen your financial acumen, and embrace the daily brew. The world of coffee awaits, ready to be transformed into a thriving business and a community hub fueled by efficiency, financial savvy, and the ever-present aroma of freshly roasted beans. Bon voyage, coffee entrepreneur! Your mobile oasis awaits, ready to blossom into a haven of deliciousness and financial success.

Building beyond the Coffee Cart:

Remember that your coffee truck is more than just a business; it's a platform for creativity, community, and personal growth.

- *Embrace your passions:* Infuse your brand with your unique interests and talents. Whether it's hosting open mic nights, showcasing local art, or offering coffee-infused recipes, find ways to express your passions and connect with your audience on a deeper level.

- *Give back to the community:* Support local causes, partner with community initiatives, or offer discounts to essential workers. Being a responsible and caring business strengthens your bond with your community and fosters goodwill.

- *Continuous learning and growth:* Never stop learning and growing! Attend workshops, participate in industry events, and connect with other coffee entrepreneurs to stay inspired, acquire new skills, and keep your business vibrant and evolving.

Remember that the true magic of your coffee truck lies in the joy of connecting with people and sharing your passion for deliciousness. Keep the coffee brewing, the connections thriving, and the learning curve ascending, and your mobile masterpiece will become more than just a business; it will become a treasured fixture in your community, a space for creativity, connection, and the ever-present joy of sharing a perfect cup of coffee.

This equips you with the knowledge and inspiration to navigate the daily grind, master financial alchemy, and build a coffee haven that thrives on both deliciousness and community. Remember, the road to coffee kingdom is paved with daily routines, financial savvy, and a generous sprinkle of passion. So, grab your beans, unleash your entrepreneurial spirit, and brew your way to success, one latte art masterpiece at a time.

Chapter 7: Coffee Odyssey: Growth & Evolution - Beyond the Beans

Chapter 7 marks a pivotal turning point in your mobile coffee saga. You've established your coffee haven, crafted your identity, and cultivated a loyal following. Now, it's time to embark on the next exciting chapter: growth and evolution. This chapter equips you with the strategies and insights to expand your reach, refine your offerings, and adapt to the dynamic world of coffee trends.

7.1 Expanding Your Coffee Cosmos: Branching Out & Diversifying

Your coffee truck is your launchpad, but the universe of caffeine beckons. In this chapter, you'll explore opportunities to branch out and diversify your business, reaching new customers and strengthening your brand.

- *Multiple locations:* One truck just isn't enough? Consider partnering with local businesses or event organizers to set up satellite coffee stations or pop-up locations, bringing your delicious brews to wider audiences.

- *Wholesale and catering:* Share the goodness! Partner with cafes, offices, or even grocery stores to offer your coffee wholesale. Cater events with your mobile haven or provide coffee and pastry platters for corporate meetings.

- *Online store and delivery:* Make it accessible! Establish an online store to offer coffee beans, merchandise, or gift baskets. Partner with delivery apps to bring your coffee directly to customers' doorsteps, catering to busy schedules and expanding your reach.

Think beyond simply multiplying your mobile units. Consider innovative ways to extend your brand and reach.

- *Subscription boxes*: Build loyalty! Offer coffee subscription boxes with curated selections, exclusive beans, or limited-edition merchandise. This fosters customer engagement and recurring revenue.

- *Workshops and coffee education:* Share your knowledge! Host coffee cupping sessions, barista training workshops, or brewing demonstration classes. Educating your customers builds brand loyalty and opens new revenue streams.

- *Collaborations and partnerships:* Cross-pollinate! Partner with complementary businesses like bakeries, food trucks, or local artists to create special collaborations, expanding your customer base and offering unique experiences.

7.2 Refining Your Roast: Menu Innovation & Customer Feedback

This chapter encourages you to continuously refine your offerings, keeping your menu fresh, exciting, and relevant to your customers' evolving preferences.

- *Seasonal specials and limited-edition drinks:* Keep it fresh! Introduce seasonal beverages and limited-edition offerings featuring unique ingredients, flavors, or brewing techniques. This fuels customer excitement and fosters a sense of anticipation.

- *Experiment and adapt:* Don't be afraid to try new things! Test new recipes, explore alternative brewing methods, or offer guest barista collaborations to introduce fresh perspectives and flavors to your menu.

- *Customer feedback and data analysis:* Listen to your beans! Pay close attention to customer feedback, monitor sales data, and conduct surveys to understand your customers' preferences and identify areas for menu improvement.

Beyond the Basics:
Go beyond simply adding new drinks to the menu. Consider unique ways to engage customers and personalize their coffee experience.

- *Customization options:* Empower your customers! Offer options for milk alternatives, sweeteners, syrups, or even cold brew infusions, allowing them to personalize their coffee to their taste.

- *Loyalty programs and rewards*: Thank your regulars! Implement a loyalty program with points, discounts, or exclusive perks to reward repeat customers and deepen their connection to your brand.

- *Social media engagement and contests:* Get interactive! Share brewing tips, customer testimonials, and behind-the-scenes glimpses on social media. Host contests and giveaways to generate excitement and brand awareness.

7.3 Embracing the Ever-Evolving Bean: Trends & Sustainability

The world of coffee is constantly evolving, and Chapter 7 helps you navigate the dynamic landscape of trends and sustainability practices.

- *Cold brew and nitro coffee:* Stay ahead of the curve! Invest in cold brew equipment and explore nitro infusions to cater to customers' growing preference for these smooth, refreshing coffee options.

- *Plant-based alternatives and sustainability*: Embrace the change! Offer plant-based milk alternatives, compostable cups and packaging, and ethically sourced beans to cater to eco-conscious customers and align with your values.

- *Technology and automation*: Embrace the future! Explore digital payment systems, online ordering platforms, or even coffee robots to streamline operations, improve customer experience, and stay ahead of the technological curve.

Beyond the Basics:
Think beyond just following trends. Be a leader in innovation and responsible practices.

- *Support local farmers and fair trade*: Source your beans responsibly! Partner with local farmers or choose fair trade coffee to ensure ethical sourcing practices and support sustainable farming communities.

- *Reduce your environmental footprint:* Implement eco-friendly initiatives like reusable cups, energy-efficient equipment, and waste reduction strategies to minimize your environmental impact.

7.3 Embracing the Ever-Evolving Bean: Trends & Sustainability

- *Community partnerships and outreach:* Be a good neighbor! Partner with local environmental organizations or participate in sustainability initiatives to showcase your commitment to responsible practices and build goodwill within your community.

- *Invest in barista training and education:* Stay ahead of the curve! Encourage your baristas to attend coffee certification courses, participate in industry events, and stay updated on emerging trends. This elevates their skills and keeps your coffee offerings at the forefront of innovation.

- *Embrace experimentation and creativity:* Foster a culture of innovation! Encourage your team to experiment with new ingredients, brewing methods, and presentation techniques. This sparks creativity, leads to unique offerings, and keeps your customers excited about what's next.

Building Beyond Basics:
Remember, growth and evolution are continuous processes. Be adaptable, embrace change, and learn from your experiences.

- *Monitor industry trends and consumer preferences:* Stay informed! Regularly research coffee trends, competitor offerings, and customer feedback to adjust your strategies and remain relevant in the dynamic coffee market.

- *Be open to feedback and criticism:* Learn and grow! Welcoming feedback from customers, baristas, and industry experts helps you identify areas for improvement and adapt your offerings to continuously deliver the best possible coffee experience.

- *Celebrate every milestone and embrace the journey:* Enjoy the ride! As your coffee truck evolves, take time to celebrate your successes, big and small. The journey of growth is filled with challenges and triumphs, and cherishing each step keeps you motivated and fuels your entrepreneurial spirit.

Brewing Beyond the Chapter: Chapter 7 has equipped you with the tools and strategies to expand your coffee universe, refine your offerings, and navigate the ever-changing landscape of coffee trends and sustainability.

From branching out to new locations to embracing eco-friendly practices, this chapter empowers you to propel your coffee truck to new heights and remain a vibrant, relevant destination for coffee connoisseurs and community enthusiasts alike. Remember, adaptability, innovation, and a commitment to ethical practices are key to sustainable growth. As you embrace the ever-evolving bean, refine your menu, and expand your reach, your mobile masterpiece will become a thriving testament to your entrepreneurial spirit and a beacon of deliciousness and social responsibility within your community.

With detailed breakdowns of diversification options, menu refinement techniques, and trend-embracing practices, you're well-equipped to transform your mobile coffee haven into a dynamic and flourishing enterprise. Remember, the journey doesn't end here – keep expanding your horizons, refining your craft, and embracing the ever-evolving bean, and your coffee truck will become a symbol of innovation, community, and the enduring love for a perfect cup of coffee.

So, raise your espresso wand, unleash your creative spirit, and embrace the endless possibilities of coffee evolution. The world of caffeine awaits, ready to be transformed into a thriving empire, one delicious innovation at a time. Bon voyage, coffee innovator! Your mobile oasis awaits, ripe for growth and ready to brew its way into the hearts and appetites of coffee lovers everywhere.

Remember that your coffee truck is more than just a business; it's a platform for social impact, environmental consciousness, and personal fulfillment.

- *Support local communities and causes*: Use your platform to make a difference! Partner with local charities, support community initiatives, or offer discounts to essential workers. Be a force for good in your community.

- *Embrace environmental sustainability:* Make conscious choices! Implement eco-friendly practices, source responsible ingredients, and advocate for sustainable consumption habits. Be a leader in environmental responsibility.

- *Nurture your team and cultivate a positive work environment:* Invest in your people! Provide opportunities for learning and growth, foster a supportive and inclusive workplace, and celebrate the collective success of your team. Happiness brews success.

This chapter is about making a positive impact on your community, embracing environmental responsibility, and fostering a thriving work environment where passion and purpose blend seamlessly. So, brew with a conscience, innovate with a heart, and grow with a team spirit, and your mobile masterpiece will become more than just a coffee haven; it will become a beacon of social impact, environmental consciousness, and the transformative power of a perfectly brewed cup of joy.

It equips you with the knowledge and inspiration to expand your coffee universe, navigate the bean's ever-evolving landscape, and create a coffee haven that thrives on deliciousness

Chapter 8: From Beans to Brand: Building a Community & Legacy - Beyond the Brews

Chapter 8 marks the final metamorphosis of your mobile coffee odyssey. You've built your haven, honed your craft, and established a loyal following. Now, it's time to transcend the boundaries of mere commerce and embark on a transformative journey of building a vibrant community and a lasting legacy around your brand. This chapter equips you with the insights and strategies to weave your coffee truck into the fabric of your community, leaving an indelible mark on hearts, taste buds, and the very notion of what a cup of coffee can represent.

8.1 Brewing Bonds: Cultivating Community & Connection

Your coffee truck is more than just a brick-and-mortar establishment; it's a space for connection, conversation, and shared experiences. You'll learn to cultivate and nurture a thriving community around your brand, fostering genuine and lasting connections with your customers and neighbors.

- *Creating a welcoming space:* Build your haven! Design your truck and surrounding area to be inviting, comfortable, and conducive to interaction. Play with lighting, music, seating arrangements, and decorative elements to create a vibrant atmosphere.

- *Hosting events and workshops:* Spark the conversation! Organize open mic nights, live music sessions, coffee cupping classes, or barista workshops. These events attract diverse audiences, create shared experiences, and breathe life into your mobile haven.

- *Embracing local partnerships:* Be a community player! Partner with local businesses, artists, or organizations to host joint events, offer co-branded products, or support community initiatives. Collaboration strengthens your presence and fosters goodwill.

Beyond the Basics:
Think beyond organized events and delve deeper into authentic connection.

- *Personalize the experience:* Remember their names! Get to know your regular customers, their preferences, and their stories. Small gestures of recognition and personalized recommendations create a sense of belonging and community.

- *Social media engagement and storytelling:* Share your journey! Utilize social media platforms to share behind-the-scenes glimpses, customer testimonials, and stories about your beans, your baristas, and your community involvement. Authenticity resonates.

- *Embrace inclusivity and accessibility:* Open your doors to everyone! Offer vegan and gluten-free options, create wheelchair-accessible spaces, and provide alternative language menus. Inclusivity fosters a welcoming environment where everyone feels valued.

8.2 Building a Legacy: Brand Storytelling & Impact

Chapter 8 empowers you to go beyond the daily grind and infuse your brand with a deeper meaning, forging a legacy that extends beyond delicious coffee.

- *Define your brand values*: Uncover your soul! Identify the core values that your brand embodies – social responsibility, environmental consciousness, artistic expression, or community spirit. These values guide your actions and resonate with like-minded customers.

- *Tell your story authentically*: Share your roots! Craft a compelling narrative about your passion for coffee, your journey as a coffee truck owner, and the values that drive your business. People connect with authenticity.

- *Partner with social causes*: Make a difference! Align your brand with causes you care about, whether it's supporting local animal shelters, participating in environmental cleanups, or donating a portion of profits to chosen charities. Your actions speak volumes.

Beyond the Basics:
Think beyond simply aligning with causes and become a catalyst for positive change.

- *Embrace sustainable practices*: Brew responsibly! Source your beans ethically, implement eco-friendly packaging, and minimize your environmental footprint. Sustainability is no longer a choice, but a necessity.

- *Empower your team and community:* Ignite the spark! Encourage your baristas to participate in community initiatives, volunteer activities, or mentor at-risk youth. Empowering others creates ripple effects of positive change.

- *Inspire through innovation:* Be a coffee pioneer! Experiment with new brewing methods, source unique ingredients, and create coffee-infused culinary experiences. Your creativity sparks trends and inspires others.

Remember, building a legacy is a continuous process. Be agile, embrace evolution, and learn from your experiences.

- *Monitor local trends and community needs:* Stay relevant! Keep abreast of community needs and emerging trends, adapting your offerings, events, and outreach initiatives to best serve your audiences.

- *Celebrate milestones and recognize achievements:* Take a moment to savor! Acknowledge the accomplishments of your team, appreciate the support of your community, and celebrate the milestones that solidify your legacy.

- *Embrace feedback and evolve with grace:* Learn and grow! Welcome constructive criticism, acknowledge setbacks as opportunities for improvement, and consistently work towards refining your brand and its impact on the community.

This chapter has equipped you with the tools and insights to transform your mobile coffee haven into a vibrant hub of community, connection, and positive impact. From fostering genuine bonds with your customers to building a legacy that resonates beyond delicious coffee, this chapter empowers you to leave an indelible mark on the hearts and minds of your community. Remember, authentic connection, purposeful storytelling, and a commitment to social responsibility are the cornerstones of a lasting legacy. As you cultivate a thriving social space, share your brand's story with authenticity, and champion causes that resonate with your values, your mobile masterpiece will transcend the realm of commerce and become a cornerstone of your community, a symbol of shared experiences, and a source of inspiration for positive change.

With detailed breakdowns of community engagement techniques, effective brand storytelling tips, and impactful social responsibility initiatives, you're well-equipped to transform your coffee haven into a beacon of connection, purpose, and positive influence. Remember, the journey doesn't end here – keep the conversations flowing, the stories unfolding, and the community thriving, and your mobile oasis will become a legacy etched not just in hearts and taste buds, but in the very fabric of your community.

So, open your doors, ignite the conversations, and embrace the transformative power of community. The world awaits, ready to connect over steaming cups of joy and witness the indelible mark you leave on your corner of the world. Bon voyage, community coffee builder! Your mobile haven awaits, poised to become a symbol of connection, impact, and the lasting legacy of a delicious dream brewed into reality.

Building Beyond the Coffee Cart:

Remember that your coffee truck is more than just a business; it's a platform for personal growth, creative expression, and a journey of self-discovery.

- *Nurture your passion and creativity:* Keep the fire burning! Experiment with new flavors, design innovative coffee experiences, and explore collaborations with local artists or musicians. Fuel your passion and keep your creative spirit alive.

- *Embrace continuous learning and growth:* Stay inquisitive! Attend industry workshops, participate in coffee conferences, and network with other entrepreneurs. Learning fuels innovation and keeps your journey exciting.

- *Give back to yourself and your community:* Share the bounty! Volunteer your time, mentor aspiring entrepreneurs, or offer discounts to those in need. Sharing your experience and resources enriches your life and strengthens your community.

This chapter is about embracing personal growth, nurturing your creative spirit, and giving back to the world around you. So, brew with passion, connect with purpose, and share your journey with generosity, and your mobile masterpiece will become more than just a coffee haven; it will become a testament to your spirit, a canvas for your creativity, and a lasting legacy of the transformative power of connection and a perfectly brewed cup of joy.

It equips you with the knowledge and inspiration to cultivate a thriving social space, leave a lasting legacy, and transform your coffee haven into a symbol of connection, purpose, and the enduring power of a delicious dream. Remember, the journey doesn't end here – keep the coffee flowing, the community thriving, and the legacy brewing, one cup of connection at a time.

So, raise your cup, open your heart, and embrace the boundless possibilities of community and legacy. The world awaits, ready to share your journey and be touched by the transformative power of your mobile masterpiece.

Bon voyage, coffee community builder! Your haven awaits, brimming with connection, purpose, and the enduring legacy of a delicious dream brewed into reality.